Poems exploring the issues
of domestic violence

f
 f
  s

Poetry and Illustrations by

Gi Dhanoa

Disclaimer

This book is designed to provide information and motivation to our readers. It is sold with the understanding that the author and publisher are not engaged to render any type of psychological, legal, or any other kind of professional advice. The content is the sole expression and opinion of its author. Neither the publisher nor the individual author(s) shall be liable for any physical, psychological, emotional, financial, or commercial damages, including, but not limited to, special, incidental, consequential or other damages. Our views and rights are the same: You are responsible for your own choices, actions, and results.

The content of the book is solely written by the author.

DVG STAR Publishing are not liable for the content of the book.

Published by DVG STAR PUBLISHING

www.dvgstar.com
email us at info@dvgstar.com

YOUR GOAL IS OUR MISSION

NO PART OF THIS WORK MAY BE REPRODUCED OR STORED IN AN INFORMATIONAL RETRIEVAL SYSTEM, WITHOUT THE EXPRESS PERMISSION OF THE PUBLISHER IN WRITING.

Copyright © 2020 Gi Dhanoa

All rights reserved.

ISBN: 1-912547-51-1
ISBN-13: 978-1-912547-51-7

For my beautiful daughter Iva Victory, my ray of sunshine, hope, joy, wisdom and my love.

May you grow and inspire with your own legacy through your dreams and aspirations to create a positive influence on the world with your sparkle.

Love

Mummy xxx

CONTENTS

Another 3

SSSSSShhhhhhhhhh 4

Help me 6

I forgot just One thing 7

Shame 8

It happened 9

Mercy 10

Unhealthy Addiction 12

Forever and Lies 13

Casually 14

Take it 15

SuFFocation 16

Coy 18

Petals 22

Island Sympathy 23

Dear Wife 24

Naive 26

Remedy 27

Moment	28
Let you	30
Call it	31
Knock Knock	32
Creature	33
Ignorance	36
No means No	38
Peaceful	40
Direction	42
Delivery	43
Flashbacks	44
Not by mistake	46
Shadow	48
No Treatment	49
Bitten	50
By	52
They don't know	54
Bruises	56
PinG pONG	57
Checkmate	58

HURTING me	60
Shattered	62
Battlefield	66
Translation	67
Killer Bee	68
Can you? & Will you?	70
Never Surrender	72
Masquerade Ball	74
First Strike	75
Chosen	76
Your Story	78
YOYo	80
Denial	83
ILLness	84
MANipulatoR	85
Captured	86
My SpOT	88
It's complicated	90
Next time	91
Do you know me better?	92

Lost 94

Final 96

Wake UP 98

Belittle me 99

Exposed 100

Suicidal self 102

Why So? 103

Who am I? 104

Intoxication 106

Thank you 107

Turning POint 108

Mother's Intuition 110

Burns 112

TEARS 114

My strength 116

I have

Forgiven what I was subjected to

Forgotten the episodes and storms I endured

Sooooo ..... now it is my time to glow

" "

Until the time is right nothing will be heard

G.D.

Another

BANG BANG BANG

tick tock
        tick tock

another strike another blow

trickle trickle splash
                      trickle trickle splash

another look another flow

duck duck breathe duck duck breathe

another excuse another sorry

BANG BANG BANG

another day another day

SSSSSShhhhhhhhhh

Ssssssshhhhhhhhhh

Don't say a word

It was an accident

You know
I didn't mean it

Don't you?

Help me

Today I screamed
I screamed
"Help me, HELP ME PLEASE"
I could not see swollen and blinded
locked myself in the bathroom
knowing this door won't hold
"Help me, help me PLEASE"
shaking and shivering
I fall to the floor
pool of tears
pool of blood
Help me, Help me Please"

I forgot just One thing

ran out in the bitter cold barefoot

and nowhere to go
ran to the top of the road

look left
                look right
and

look ahead

oh damn
I just forgot one thing
looked behind
rewound my steps
now it's back to the front door
oh damn
I just forgot
one
thing

Shame

I see the fusion
blue green purple and maroon
I pick up the brush
and begin to disguise
but
the storm of tears
f
l
o
w
I don't see me
no more
no
more
I have been swallowed in by shame

It happened

It only happened once
So it must be ok
Maybe it was stress
Maybe it was my giggle
Maybe it was because I forgot to smile
Maybe it was the room
Maybe it was my shoes
It only happened once
So
surely
It's
O
K

Mercy

Engulfed in your mercy
Victory no more
War is on the horizon
Build your walls
Weak weapons at the ready
Breathe the stale air
And
Victory no more
No more
Just hold me
As
I
Lay here

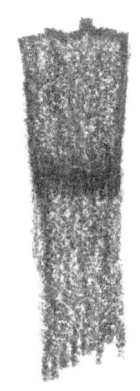

Unhealthy Addiction

I fly
I whirl
I catch onto another
Short term relief
But
Still
I am trying to find my way back
To
YOU

Forever and Lies

I remember

You pretended   I forgave

You begged   I listened

You begged

AGAIN   I listened

You cried   I forgave

AGAIN

Forever and Lies

AGAIN

Casually

No longer
Can I say?
Or tell
What is going on?
Between us

Casually our situation has
Just
Become routine
For
Us

BUT
I am j u s t
anticipating
For the chaNGE
To give my
Confused
Emotions
A chance to express
Instead of being
Suppressed

Take it

I see now

That

YOU

Can't take

IT

When

I AM READY

I will be

Taking

NONE

OF

IT

SuFFocation

Suffocated by the warmth air around me

Burnt by the hot bulb burning

Seventy percent blocks of white

Twenty percent splashes of brown

A ten most important percent of clutter

Clutter in my head

Clutter in my cell

Brown is for escape

But I will never

Open that door

Coy

I felt I was blooming
Glowing in our spark
Didn't realise I was the igniter
The solo starter
And the only player
In your games

Coy you played
Deceived by
Your eyes
Your smiles
And
Words
You spoke out ALOUD

Openly you misled
Slimey Lies
And fake news
Ringing in my ears
All that is left and
WHAT
I will remember
NOW
Of   YOU

" "

When you find yourself amongst the dirt and on the cold floor that will be your best time to re-establish and grow back with a remarkable inner strength and glow.

G.D.

Petals

One
By
One

You

Would

Remove my petals

Leave me bare with no comfort

Then

Left OUTSIDE

in the making of your

STORM

Island Sympathy

Hop

Island
                     to
                                   Island

Looking for your victim

Who will swallow your stories

Whilst you show no pride

Hop

                                        Island
                                              to
                                                       Island

Looking for your next victim

Dear Wife

I am so sorry for the way I behaved

I don't know what came over me

It was when you started to nag

It was when you pointed your finger

It was when you sniggered

It was when you laughed

It was that dress

It was because you said no

I am sorry

Please come back

I Love You

Your Husband xxx

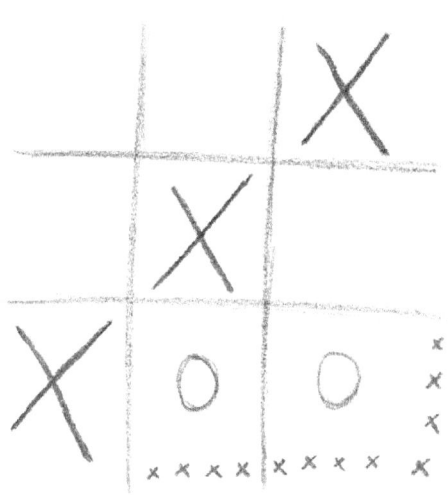

Naive

Unaware of your past

I

Believe all you have to say

I

Experience the wonderful lifestyle

I

Partake in the partying and the games

I

Forgive a few incidents

I

Take the blame

Remedy

Telling me your lies
Showing me your cries
Feeding me your poison

Invaded my soul and being

Now I am fighting

To find a remedy

That would exclude

your presence

and

your existence

Moment

Yesterday I gave
You openly received

Today you deceived
So I walk

A
  W
    A
      Y

Let you

Silently I cry over you

&

Then I am ashamed

Of

What I let you

put

ME through

Call it

You call it an obsession

I call it confusion

You get annoyed

I call it hiding

You walk off

I stay up

Waiting for this uncertainty

To slide

Knock Knock

Every Knock
Is NOT
Worth opening
the door for

Some should
Continue
Knocking

Until it becomes
A
DISTant
Echo

Echoooooo

Creature

I was eluded for tooooooooooo long

I did not even know myself anymore

Who is this creature? I ask myself

Peering at my reflection in my silver water bowl

So colourless and lifeless

Limbs barely working

Who is this creature? I ask myself

" "

When you believe that will never be you, take a pause,

close your eyes and imagine that is you.

G.D.

·

Ignorance

My purity exposed before you

caught your attention

My joy and energy

encapsulated you

My love and warmth

protected you

My smiles and solidarity

shielded your truth

No means No

If I say

No thank you

Not today

I mean what I say

No

Means

No

" "

Knowledge and teachings to abolish suppression and violence.

G.D.

Peaceful

I want to fly away

Where the sky

Does not cry

&

Where the moon

Just

ShineS

Direction

My beautiful struggle

      P

U

The road

No turning

              LEFT

Or

                RIGHT

For help

Delivery

No stir

No sound

No warning

That today

Would have been

My day

To become

A delivery

Back home

In my own box

Flashbacks

If   I   take   myself   there

Which is not often

I   close   my eyes

And I see you

Outraged monster consumed
By ANGER and VIOLENCE

I see you on that final day
To what was considered home

Reached for your weapon
To attempt your
Final
BLOW

Not by mistake

I am here
Beside you
Not by mistake

Look at me
Notice ME
I am still H   E   R   E

Forgotten now
Years have passed
I am still here

W   A   I   T   I   N   G

.

" "

Smiles build Solidarity

G.D.

Shadow

The shadow may have returned

Now back in my life

BUT

I will not

GIVE UP

I WILL

SIT UP

&

CONTINUE

MY PATH

TOWARDS

MY NEW LIFE

No Treatment

Misguided

Used

&

Abused

Now the soul has E
                      R
                            O
                                    D
                                           E
                                                    D

Bitten

Pierce my skin

Mark my skin

Create a wound

That you are proud

To call

Yours

By

I am wounded by the words
I am wounded by the actions
I am wounded by what comes after

I am wounded by your presence
I am wounded by your stare
I am wounded by your intentions

I am wounded by the guilt you place

I am wound by YOU

" "

Love is not having a hold over your partner, but

encouraging them to grow without you

as much as with you.

G.D.

They don't know

I dread going home
I   w   a   l   k
as
s   l   o   w
as I can
I have to hide
She is waiting
ready
1st Shout
steady
2nd slap
go
3rd punch
They don't know

Bruises

Green

Pink

Purple

Yellow

Maroon

Black

Brown

Red

Amber

Orange

Blue

PinG pONG

P   P

 ING   ONG

         P   ING

P

            ONG

               P   P

            ING   ONG

Checkmate

Struggling

Anticipating

Your next move

As it could be

my
last

HURTING me

Please don't do that again

I told you the last time

how you are

HURTING me

Please don't do that again

I told you the time before last

how you are

HURTING me

Please don't

Please STOP

" "

Never forget you and your identity within a relationship,

there is nothing more beautiful than

parallel blossoming.

G.D.

Shattered

Exhausted and consumed by your
In   con sis   ten c   y
Confused and misled
Exposed and vulnerable
To another episode
Another time
Secret cry
A panic
A SHOCK
Just
Shatt
       ered

" "

I openly forgive you and forget you to ensure I live my

life to the fullest.

Whilst you figure out what happened!

G.D.

Battlefield

Weakened

Tired

Exhausted

Of this fight

No longer

Do I wish to take part

In this battle

That has long lost

Its purpose

That has long lost

Its meaning

Translation

A moment

That once seemed so real

Was not a promise of forever

Instead one of

CAUTION

&

neglect

Killer Bee

Killer Killer Killer

Bee

Raging and buzzing

Around me

Killer Killer Killer

Bee

Steaming and seething

Ready to attack

Killer Killer Killer

Bee

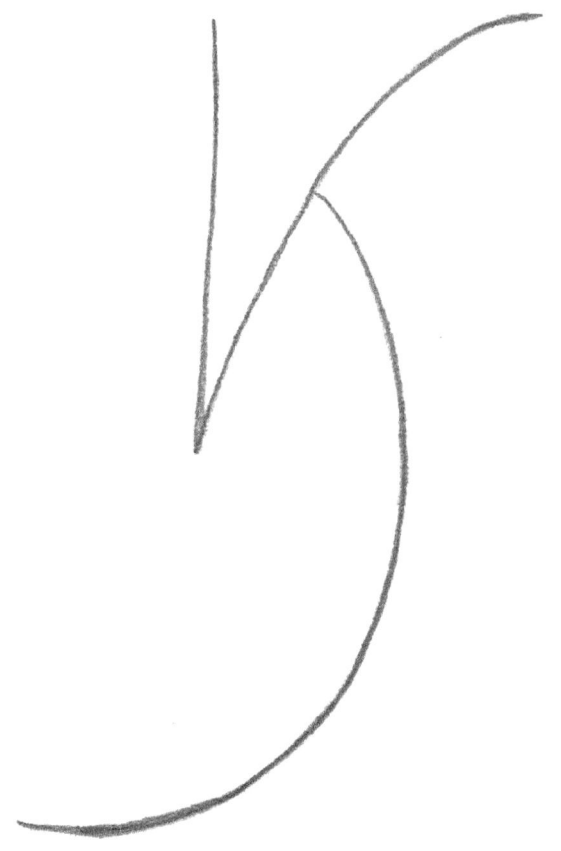

Can you? & Will you?

Can you understand?
Will you ever understand?

Can you learn what you have?
Will you ever learn what you have?

Can you be pure?
Will you ever be pure?

Can you love?
Will you ever love?

Can you? & Will you?

" "

When that feeling is telling you to do it........flee,

listen to it and don't look back.

G.D.

Never Surrender

Never ever will I fully
Surrender

I was losing my battle
But continued to remain

Never ever will I fully
Surrender

To those wolves hiding
In the forest that obstruct my way

Never ever will I fully
Surrender

Never

Ever

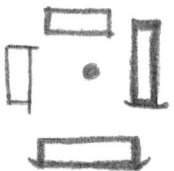

Masquerade Ball

I appear in my disguise
To share an evening with you all
To indulge in laughter and joy
And create new memories of happiness

As I dance the night away
High on my new found life

I suddenly feel a familiar hold
One of control and aggression
Whispers of promises
Of
Broken bones
When we return
Home

First Strike

I packed my life up
Like a snail

Crossed the seas
And came home

Underestimated the danger
Still I came

There to support
And help you get better

Howling wind
And shutters are flapping

You raise your hand
And crush the little snail

Welcome home
&
Thank you for coming

Chosen

Am I
      H
            E
                  R
                          E
                              to feel the pain?
To encompass the

Be
      trayal

Your Story

I heard your story
I couldn't believe it to be true

It remained at the back of my mind
Unknown to me

I would become you
Feel your pain
First hand
Beg for my life
As you did

I became you

the main character

in

Your story

" "

Is a lingering promise a weakness of lack of happening

in the now?

G.D.

Y
O
Y
o

I believe I am stuck
Within your circumference
Round and Round
I tread on the ride of what has become
MY CHOSEN LIFE

I believe I am stuck
Treading on eggshells
Awaiting
For the
next moment
next episode
next play

I believe I am stuck

" "

When my gut speaks, I now make time to listen and reschedule my plans to connect with that inner feeling of sense and wisdom. Which is so often right, but ignored.

G.D.

Denial

Pretending it's not happening

Is that denial?

Not talking about it

Is that denial?

Covering up my wounds

Is that denial?

Smiling when in pain

Is that denial?

What is denial?

ILLness

Overtaken and possessed
By an invisible illness
Unable to comprehend
Unable to express
A taboo within your
Cultural society

soooooooooooooooooooo

Keep it vented in
Take it out on someone
Close instead

I am unable to comprehend

What now is yours?
&
Our life

Or

what now isn't
Yours
& Our life

MANipulatoR

Now fully aware

Of what your games consisted of

The guilt

The blame

The pointing

The lack

The hurt

Goodbye MANipulatoR

Captured

In desperation
I have begun to pluck my own feathers

In desperation
I stop singing my morning song

In desperation
I refuse to migrate to warmer climates

In desperation
I stare in my captor's eyes

Pleading for mercy

&

Forgiveness for my unknown sins

" "

As difficult as it feels in that moment in time,

detoxification is vital for your soul and growth.

Let go of what is causing you pain and holding you back.

G.D.

My SpOT

Livid
Frustrated
SCREAming

I knew my place amongst the cold bricks

B   R   O   K   E   N

Collapsed

On the floor again

OVER POWERED StruGGle

Hopeless

&

D
R
A
I
N
E
D

It's complicated

Yes I hear you

Yes you have your opinion

Yes I hear you

Yes things need to change

Yes it's not working

Yes I hear you

It's just

It's just

That

 it's complicated

Next time

When it happens again

I promise

Next time

I will

leave

Do you know me better?

I see you

Gathering at the corners

Judging and gossiping

About last night's drama

In my home

Did I ask for your opinions?

Did I ask for you to share out aloud?

Did I ask you to check on me this morning?

All you need to know he loves me and I love him and

that is all you need to know

Lost

Lost within your love

        Once knew myself without you

Numb whilst you talk at me

        Excited to take the bins OUT

Rescue me Rescue me

RESCUE ME   RESCUE ME   RESCUE ME

" "

When you feel you are no longer coping, that in fact is your turning point of realisation. A triumphant and significant moment of hope.

G.D.

Final

She

screams

for

her

MUM

In her last breath

Wake UP

It's a gorgeous day outside

BUT

I DON'T WANT TO

Wake UP

I have a lovely day planned

BUT

I DON'T WANT TO

Wake UP

Sharing myself
Is just too much

So I am not going to

Wake UP

Belittle me

I stood before you vulnerable
Lacking self esteem
My own past not your fault
But still I believed

You smiled and took me under your wing
snuggled a little and kept me still

Safe it felt for a year
until I believed I could grow

So came the remarks and games
Belittling me became part of everyday

Searching for those snuggles that once were

Now replaced by

Mental torture

    &   DEPARTure

Exposed

I am
Attracted to your glow and glisten
Addicted
To that joy and pleasure of a high
I remain
I wait
I am exposed
NOW
I am numb
I am cold
You did not GLOW today

Suicidal self

NOW has come the time
I can no longer

PRETEND

NOW has come the time
I have chosen

ESCAPE

NOW has come the time
I know it's

TIME

NOW has come the time
To say

GOODBYE

Why So?

Why So?
After we fought for this justice
Of beautiful celebration
Two of the same to be as one

Why So?
Would you then punish me
After I have committed
My ALL to				YOU

Why So?
Can we not live in harmony
As promised on that day

Why So?
Does your jealousy
Harm me in the name of

     LO   VE

Who am I?

My identity entangled

My reputation in shatters

My face unrecognisable

My esteem invisible

Who am

I?

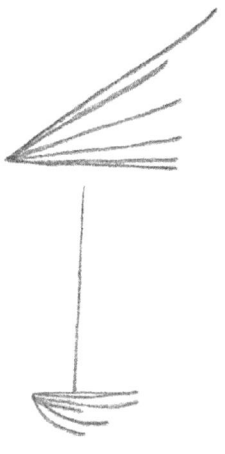

Intoxication

Together we blame

it on the intoxication

make up and continue

The chILdren blame and are unable to forgive

US

and

the PoisoN

 for their internal and external

ScaRS

Thank you

Thank you for being part of my journey

without those moments

I would not be

ME

      and

I love me

Thank you

Turning POint

You asked me to look in the
MIRROR
RORRIM

Do I see myself at 50?
Living this same unhappy life?

Truth be told
I didn't see myself in the mirror
at 50

I would have expired long before had I stayed

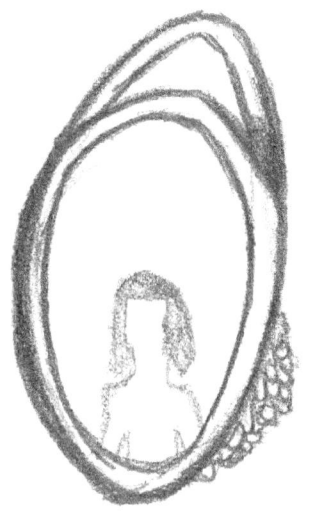

Mother's Intuition

Call it a sixth sense
Or a mother's intuition

You knew
I was fading
Before you

Not speaking the truth
Not speaking at all anymore

You knew
I was hiding
You knew
I was hurting
You Knew
I was eroding

Call it a sixth sense
Or a mother's intuition

" "

Allowing the full demolition, the permission to destroy something already broken, was the best decision I made.

G.D.

Burns

I was told

I will remain

BeaUtiful

With my forever

ScarS

YOU have chosen

To place on MY body

Without MY permission

Without MY consent

Burns you told me

are beautiful

" "

There were times when the freedom of darkness, was more desirable than enduring the pain one more day.

G.D.

TEARS

Falling and sparkling
Like diamonds crashing
On the concrete floor
Valuable
Precious
Memories
Shattered
Erased by sirens
Elevated by my saviours
Of
HOPE

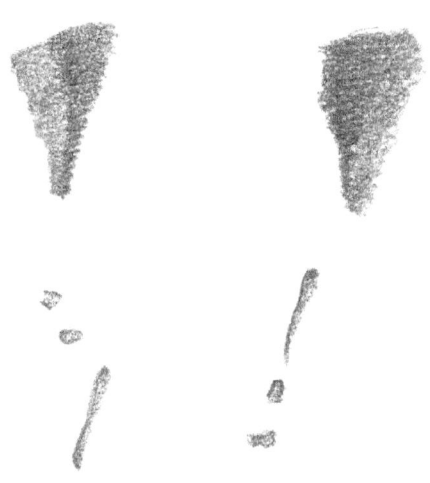

My strength

If it wasn't for my strength

My expressive words

My quick thinking

My emotive eyes

I would have been history

in this distant territory

" "

I knew this was not in vain; my experiences with you. I knew I was growing and rooting myself for something much bigger.

G.D.

Thank you for travelling through the turmoil journey of what is known as Domestic and Mental Abuse within a toxic relationship.

May you find the strength, support and courage to speak up if you ever found yourself in a vulnerable state of being a receiver of abuse.

It never just happens once,

it's a build up

leading to

a destructive path

of YOU.

YOU DESERVE BETTER

ENOUGH = ENOUGH

My Favourite Poems

-
-
-
-
-

Poems that touched me

-
-
-
-
-

Poems that inspired me

-
-
-
-
-

Poems that made me feel

-
-
-
-
-

Notes

Notes

Notes

Notes

If you wish to share or get in touch to how this book has positively influenced you and your situation to take the first steps of action.

I would love to hear from you

@ffs_g.d.poetry

FFS_g.d.poetry

www.ingramcontent.com/pod-product-compliance
Lightning Source LLC
LaVergne TN
LVHW021118080426
835508LV00037B/3113